The World's Deadliest

The Deadliest Plants on Earth

by Connie Colwell Miller

Reading Consultant:
Barbara J. Fox
Reading Specialist
North Carolina State University

Content Consultant:
Jerry Davis, PhD
Honorary Fellow
Department of Botany
University of Wisconsin, Madison

CAPSTONE PRESS
a capstone imprint

Blazers is published by Capstone Press,
151 Good Counsel Drive, P.O. Box 669, Mankato, Minnesota 56002.
www.capstonepress.com

Library of Congress Cataloging-in-Publication Data
Miller, Connie Colwell, 1976–
    The deadliest plants on earth / by Connie Colwell Miller.
    p. cm. — (Blazers. The world's deadliest)
    Summary: "Describes deadly plants and what makes them dangerous" — Provided
by publisher.
    Includes bibliographical references and index.
    ISBN 978-1-4296-3933-0 (library binding)
    1. Poisonous plants — Juvenile literature. 2. Dangerous plants — Juvenile literature. I. Title.
II. Series: Blazers. World's deadliest.
QK100.A1M55 2010
581.6'59 — dc22   2009026654

Editorial Credits
Christopher L. Harbo, editor; Matt Bruning, designer; Svetlana Zhurkin, media researcher;
    Laura Manthe, production specialist

Photo Credits
Alamy/blickwinkel, 25; botanikfoto/Steffen Hauser, 7, 13; Chinju@digipix, 23; tbkmedia, 21
iStockphoto/8651096, 10; Bogdan Radenkovic, cover (seeds); Hubert Inabinet, 27; Jivko
    Kazakov, 29; Margo vanLeeuwen, 5
Peter Arnold/H. Reinhard, 16; The Medical File/Medicimage, 19
Shutterstock/arteretum, cover (leaves), 1; Chas, 9; Eduard Andras, 15; Thomas Fredriksen,
    cover (algae texture)

TABLE OF CONTENTS

DEADLY PLANTS

Beware of killer plants! That sounds like a joke, but it's not. The plants in this book look beautiful, but they can kill. Check out some of the deadliest plants on earth.

Monkshood

SORT OF DANGEROUS

DEADLY PETALS

Mountain death camas have beautiful white flowers. But this pretty plant is dangerous to sheep, cattle, and horses. Mountain death camas cause drooling, **vomiting**, and even death in animals.

vomit – to throw up food and liquid from the stomach through the mouth

SOUR MILK

Cows that eat too much snakeroot plant produce **poisonous** milk. Meat from these cows can also become poisoned. This poisoned milk and meat cause vomiting, trembling, and terrible pain. Milk sickness can kill people.

DEADLY *FACT*

Abraham Lincoln's mother died of milk sickness.

poisonous – harmful if swallowed, inhaled, or touched

9

SMELLS SWEET

The angel's trumpet plant smells sweet. But it is actually quite dangerous. Eating this plant can cause painful **seizures** and even death.

seizure – uncontrollable twitching of a muscle or muscles

DEADLY SAP

Bushman's poison produces sweet-smelling flowers and tasty berries. But animals that swallow the **sap** from this plant can die.

DEADLY FACT

South African bushmen used this plant's sap to make poison dart tips. The darts were used to hunt animals for food.

sap – a liquid that flows up and down inside a plant

13

Chapter 3
VERY
DANGEROUS

BAD FOR YEW!

Every part of the yew tree is poisonous, except the berries. But eating these bright red berries is dangerous. Very poisonous seeds are inside them.

BERRY POISONOUS

Deadly nightshade grows plump, black berries. Just two nightshade berries can kill a small child. The leaves and roots of this plant are also poisonous.

DEADLY *FACT*

Deadly nightshade is also called belladonna.

CHOKED UP!

Stay away from the seeds of the strychnine (STRICK-nine) plant. Eating these seeds can cause painful vomiting and seizures. People can stop breathing and die after eating the deadly seeds.

DEADLY FACT

Historians believe Egypt's Queen Cleopatra killed her own servants. She forced them to eat strychnine seeds.

PANIC ATTACK

The leaves and stems of monkshood are poisonous. Eating this plant causes burning in the mouth and then vomiting. People can even stop breathing.

DEADLY *FACT*

People can be poisoned just by touching monkshood.

Chapter 4

EXTREMELY DANGEROUS

PEA POISON

Rosary pea seeds are easy to spot. A single black dot marks each bright red seed. Eating the seeds causes vomiting, **fever**, and even death.

fever – a body temperature that is higher than normal

DEADLY FACT

One rosary pea seed may contain enough poison to kill an adult!

KILLER SAP

The flowers and stems of the pretty water hemlock are safe. But the roots are full of sap that causes seizures and death. Even a tiny amount of sap can kill.

DEADLY FACT

Water hemlock can kill a cow in as little as 15 minutes!

Hemlock root

SMOKED OUT!

Eating just one leaf of the oleander plant can kill. In fact, simply touching the twigs, **blooms**, and berries can poison people.

DEADLY FACT

Even smoke from burning oleander wood is poisonous!

bloom – a flower on a plant

DEADLY BEAN

Eating just one tiny castor bean can kill a child within minutes. As few as eight beans could kill an adult. Whether it's beans, seeds, or sap, many plants pack a deadly punch.

GLOSSARY

bloom (BLOOM) — a flower on a plant

fever (FEE-vur) — a body temperature that is higher than normal

poisonous (POI-zuhn-uhss) — able to kill or harm if swallowed, inhaled, or sometimes even touched

sap (SAP) — the liquid that flows up and down inside a plant carrying water and food from one part of the plant to another

seizure (SEE-zhur) — uncontrollable twitching of a muscle or muscles

vomit (VOM-it) — to throw up food and liquid from the stomach through the mouth

READ MORE

Day, Jeff. *Don't Touch That!: The Book of Gross, Poisonous, and Downright Icky Plants and Critters.* Chicago: Chicago Review Press, 2008.

Johnson, Rebecca L. *Carnivorous Plants.* Nature Watch. Minneapolis: Lerner, 2007.

Preszler, June. *Meat-Eating Plants and Other Extreme Plant Life.* Extreme Life. Mankato, Minn.: Capstone Press, 2008.

INTERNET SITES

FactHound offers a safe, fun way to find Internet sites related to this book. All of the sites on FactHound have been researched by our staff.

Here's all you do:

Visit *www.facthound.com*

FactHound will fetch the best sites for you!

INDEX